with David Bellamy

ON A TRAIN JOURNEY

I-Spy Books
12 Star Road, Partridge Green
Horsham, Sussex RH13 8RA

Everybody loves going on trains. They take you to places you've never been to before, and show you lots of exciting things on the way. *I-SPY on a Train Journey* tells you some of the things you will see – trains and track, signals and sidings, fast, modern trains, old slow ones and even old fast ones too. Anything in fact you may see on your journey.

Railway spotting is fun, but there is a serious side to it too. Don't take any chances that might lead to an accident; never put your head out of the train window, and always keep on the right side of railway fences. Trespassing is not only illegal, it is very dangerous.

SCORING

When your scores total 1,250 points you may award yourself the rank of TRAIN TRAVELLER Second Class. When they reach a complete total of 1,500 points you are entitled to the rank of TRAIN TRAVELLER First Class; you may then send your book to me, and I shall return it to you stamped with my personal seal. Your certificate of rank is on the inside back cover of this book.

There are 10,706 route miles of railway track in this country, 2,700 stations, 3,016 locomotives and 14,661 carriages. Every train, every mile of track, every journey you take will show you something new about railways. It might be an unusual notice, a named-train, or simply a stretch of countryside you've never seen before.

Our railways are changing all the time. More is being spent on modernization. So you'll often see the old and the new together, like these two stations for instance. The Birmingham International (1) station opened in 1976, and the Achnasheen Station, Inverness (2) typically old-fashioned station that you'll see in many parts of the country.

Which station did you visit? ....

Did it have a foundation stone or date mark? ...
....Score **50**

Ticket office Look out for main (3) or suburban line ticket offices; the number of the window; the class and destination number; the notice giving conditions of sale for tickets. Really up-to-date ticket offices are streamlined for efficiency. In big stations destinations are listed alphabetically and you must choose the right window for where you want to go.

Look through the window at the tubes or hoppers holding hundreds of tickets. You may speak to the ticket clerk through a hole in a window, a grille. A louvred window, a hygiaphone (3) prevents the spread of infection. SPY new ticket machines APTIS and PORTIS.

What else did you notice about the ticket office you saw? ....Score **40**

(4)

(5)

There's so much to see at every station (4). At the bigger ones you might see a photograph booth, shops, stamp machines, Rail Drive (5).

Look out also for the station clock, statues and plaques, left-luggage lockers, *Bureau de change* and more.

What else unusual did you see on the platform?

It had phones and ....

photographs. .... Score **30**

(6)

Train departure boards

Not all departure boards are like this one at Euston (6). It shows arrivals as well as departures, uses digital clocks and is computer operated. At smaller stations departures can be announced over loudspeakers and shown on electronic boards on each platform. At one time boards were wooden and slotted into a rack on the wall by the station manager before the arrival of each train.

How did you find out which platform your train was leaving from? .... Score **30**

There are other ways of getting information. I-SPY timetables on walls or stands (7), information desks or Travel Centres. In the Travel Centre you can book your journey in advance, including those by sea or air. At Kings Cross Travel Centre in London there is a computer which gives information (8). In and around the station you might also see station signs, perhaps in old tiles, or in the modern style.

Which sign interested you? ....Score **20**

(7)

(8)

On the platform

You might see working: a BRUTE (9) British Rail Universal Trolley – for post and parcels; they are always painted blue. (10) is an all-purpose electric truck. Red trolleys belong to the Post Office for Royal Mail traffic.

Red Star service takes parcels on journeys more quickly than by post. It is put on a train at the beginning of a journey and can be collected an hour after it reaches its destination, from the Red Star office at the station.

Look for self-help trollies (11) or the electric truck pulling a fresh water container to or from a train about to leave, or a platform sweeper.

What else did you see on the platform? ....
Saw a train person
....Score **30**
shutting all the door

SPY all the notices in the station. Here is a common one (12) but there are many others, you may even SPY an old one.

(10)
Tickets
Red Star Parcels
Staff only this side
Red Star Traffic
JGK 345K

(11)

(12)
Way out
Tickets
Luggage
lockers

Uniforms and jobs

Could you tell a railman from a driver, or a chargeman from a supervisor?

Railman Navy blue coat, or blouson jacket, with red frame collar trim, blue-grey trousers. Red BR symbol near the top of the sleeves and red rank markings above cuffs. Navy blue hat with red band and BR symbol. Station maintenance, cleaner and loader.

Leading railman Similar uniform to railman. Ticket collector, announcer; also issues tickets.

Senior railman As for Railman but with blue frame trim on the collar, and blue rank markings, navy blue hat has blue band and BR symbol. Ticket collector.

Chargeman As for Senior Railman. SPY him on larger stations, in charge of the men above.

Driver What does he wear? ....Score **30**

Guard Blue-grey jacket or coat, silver buttons and silver coloured rank markings on the sleeve. 'Guard' badge and silver coloured BR symbol collar badges on slate-grey background. Navy blue trousers, light blue shirts. Blue-grey hat with grey side flag, silver coloured trim and BR symbol.

Train crew supervisor Blue-grey jacket and trousers, gold coloured BR symbols on sleeves and cap. 'Supervisor' badge, gold coloured on blue-grey background. Blue-grey cap. White shirts, navy blue tie with BR symbol.

Railwomen, female guards, chargewomen etc., wear same uniforms as the men, but may have blue-grey skirts.

Rail air Hostess Light grey suits; silver rail-air

link badge on breast pocket on navy-blue background. Matching badge on light grey hat with grey band. Black leather shoulder bag. SPY her on rail/air changeover stations. Notice the platform supervisor (13) is holding a lamp rather than a flag. Conductor guard (14)

What did you notice about the buttons on the uniform you saw? .... Score **20**

(13)

(14)

Modern **ticket barriers** tell you simply and efficiently the number of the platform, the time of departure of the next train and where it stops. Your ticket barrier might be a sliding, concertina gate or like (15). By it you may find the information on a board (16). Look out for the platform ticket machine; it will give you a ticket to go on to the platform but not to travel on the train.

Once on the platform you'll probably see **buffers**, hydraulic ones (17) operated by water, or fixed buffers made of thick beams of wood or pieces of rail, or the concertina type.

Where did you see buffers? ....

What type? ....Score **30**

It's surprising how much you can learn about the engine that's pulling your train, or the carriage in which you're sitting, just by looking closely at them before the train sets off.

On the side of a diesel is a plaque (18). It tells you its class, weight, maximum speed and its RA – Route Availability. The RA of a locomotive tells British Rail officials what sort of route the loco can operate on. Some tracks, for instance, might have bends too sharp or bridges too weak.

On the ends of your carriage you will probably see a restriction notice – it means virtually the same as RA for a loco. You'll also find out how fast it's allowed to go, how it is heated, its size, weight and date of construction.

Name one fact about your carriage that you discovered ....Score **60**

(15)

NEXT TRAIN FROM THIS PLATFORM
POOLE
CALLING AT
READING BASINGSTOKE WINCHESTER
SOUTHAMPTON BOURNEMOUTH
(16)

2K01
Moorgate
313003
(18)

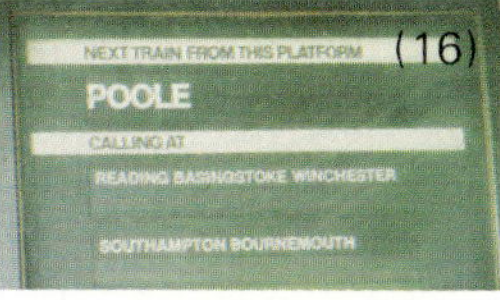

(17)

Here are some types of 'pulling power' or traction used by British Rail. Traction can be provided by single units called locomotives, or multiple units which have power incorporated in the passenger unit car.

1 The Class 141 (19 is a 140) or railbus DMU (Diesel Mechanical Unit) has no separate engine, but has 2 powered coaches. It can be driven from either end so it can reverse at the end of the journey without having to be shunted. They are found on rural routes; you can most likely see them in South West Yorkshire.

2 Class 317 EMU (electric multiple unit) (20). They have no guard on board, the driver checks that it is safe to move the train from the station by means of a television screen on the platform linked to a camera. SPY EMUs on busy commuter routes. Electric trains may take power from an overhead catenary system by means of its pantograph, or as on Southern Region, by means of 'shoes' which take power from a live conductor laid alongside the 2 running rails.

3 Other locos such as class 47, 50 are diesel-powered, they are noisier.

4 Locos tend to be used on longer journeys. They can haul up to 15 coaches. The class 87 (21) electric loco has a maximum speed of 176 kph.

What sort of loco was pulling your train? ....
....Score **50**

A different sort of loco is the diesel shunting loco (22). It takes coaches and freight wagons short distances to sidings or other tracks.

(19)

(20)

(22)

(21)

The InterCity 125 **High Speed Train** – speed for the eighties! It operates on over 50% of all InterCity Services. There are 95 such trains on the Eastern, Western, London, Midland and Scottish regions, travelling at 200 kph (125 mph). In fact the HST holds the world record for the fastest diesel traction 229 kmp (143 mph). It is very often the curvature of the track which restricts the speed of a train, rather than its power. Here is one InterCity livery (23).

Coaches

Special coaches are the 'sleepers' (24) which have smaller windows. This one is at Kings Cross Station. If it is early in the morning the passengers may still be sleeping, as they don't have to leave the train when it first arrives.

Where did you see a sleeper? ....Score **60**

Mark III carriages (25) are air-conditioned, working on British Rail's fastest routes. Because it is air-conditioned, compartment windows do not open – the temperature inside the carriage is automatically controlled. This carriage has wrap-round doors at the end which give a wider space when opened, making entry with a suitcase much simpler. Earlier coaches are very similar and more common, also with wrap-round doors; not air-conditioned though, so compartments have quarter windows which open.

Mark III carriages are longer (22 metres) than the older Mark II ones (20 metres) and take more passengers.

What was the number of your carriage? ....
....Score **30**

(23)

(24)

(25)

Numbers

Each loco has a number on its side. The first two numbers show the class – or power range – to which the loco belongs; the remaining numbers are given as the loco leaves the works. A loco numbered 87008 (26) means that it's the eighth one of its class to be made.

Engines used to have headcodes on the front. The space is now taken up by windows or lights. You may, however, still see them and 2 number codes on Southern Region trains.

The signalman used to read the headcode to identify the train that was approaching the signal box. Now they know which train is coming from lights on a panel in their signal box. The train passing over a part of the track activates a signal which is carried to the signal box electronically. The track circuit means they need never look out of the window at the trains, and so modern signal boxes have few windows. The driver receives signals too, from the track, which act as warnings on the line ahead.

On locos and carriages you will see many other numbers too, which indicate class, weight etc.

What numbers have you seen on a loco or carriage and what did they mean? ....

.... Score **70**

You may see these inside the carriage (1) Toilet sign (2) A plate explaining where and when the carriage was made (3) A light switch for use by guards (4) First class sign (5) Fire extinguisher (6) 'No-smoking' signs and alarm cord.

(26)

Signal Boxes Old (27), new (28). The old type are smaller, more easily recognisable, built of wood and house heavy signal apparatus which is cumbersome to control.

New signal boxes are built of modern materials – steel, concrete and glass – and house modern signalling apparatus, simple and easy to control. The signalman presses switches instead of pulling levers. In the old days he had to pull a separate lever for each set of points and for each signal; now he has to press only one or two switches to pass a train through a whole set of points at a junction. This is called route setting. The signalman selects the route for a train and works the switches for that particular route.
There are fewer and fewer signal boxes, as new boxes often do the work of many and control points many kilometres away.
Where did you see your signal box? ....
Was it old or new? ....Score **10**

Ground Disc signal A You will see either a black or a red horizontal bar across it, and a flood-light above. It is generally used for shunting.

Banner repeating signals B These are used to repeat semaphore signals which are difficult to see.

Shunting signal C Shunting signals in general control trains passing from a siding to a running line or vice versa, as well as from one running line to another.

(27)

Etchingham

(A)

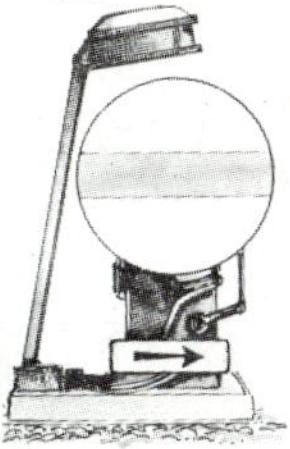

(B)

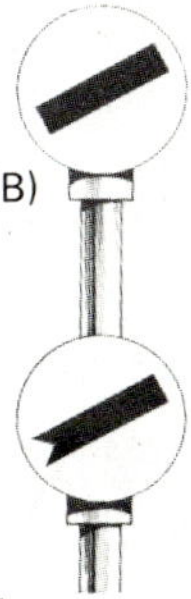

(C)

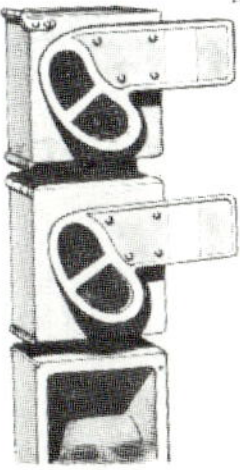

Signals
Modern signals are coloured lights (29), the old semaphore ones are becoming rare.

Colour light signals they show up better in all weathers. There are three main types:
Two aspect: red and green
Three aspect: red, yellow and green
Four aspect: red, two yellow and green

Four aspect colour light running signals: for busy lines, as extra caution.

Red: stop
One yellow: caution – prepare to stop at next signal.
Two yellows: next signal is at caution and the one after that at stop
Green: all clear

Which colour light signals have you seen and where? ......red in London...... Score **30**

Three-aspect light signal (30)
Note: Wire mesh shields to protect staff from overhead wires
Three-aspect colour light signal
Station and signal number
Train starting indicator (may say: RA, right of way)
Route indicator (may say: ML, main line)
Telephone for the driver to speak to the signalman.

Where have you seen a three-aspect light signal with route indicator? ......London...... Score **50**

More Signals

Position light ground signal (31). Used for shunting purposes. Two horizontal lights (one red, one white) indicate stop. Two illuminated white lights at 45 degrees mean proceed.

Where have you seen a position light ground signal? Charing Cross ....Score **80**

Which route would you take from where you live to get to Gatwick or Heathrow Airport? Some stations are inside airports, as at Gatwick (32) or there are coach links as at Reading (33).

You can make connections with other countries by sea – hovercraft, jetfoil or ship.

Gatwick – London trains have a special livery (34).

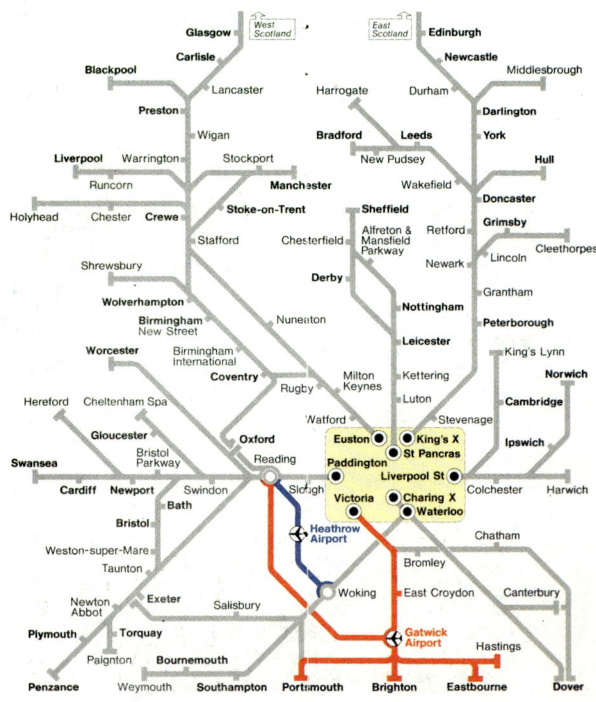

(32)

(33)

(34)

More Signals

Semaphore signals are much harder to understand than the coloured lights system. The powerful lights can be seen over 1 km away even in bad weather, giving the fastest train time to stop. The front cover picture has 2 signals, one for the main route, one for a loop. It is on the Plymouth-Penzance line.

There were 2 types of signal: STOP; square-ended, red with white band; and DISTANT; fish-tailed, yellow with black band. With these two a bewildering combination of messages could be relayed, all telling the driver what to do.

Where did you see semaphore signals? ....

.... Score **70**

Signs along tracks

Look for mileposts along the offside track at quarter mile intervals. They may be yellow but there are many different kinds (35).

What sort of milestone did you see? ....

.... Score **20**

Gradient Post (36) You will see this post where the rail does not run on completely flat ground. The number gives the gradient – in this case it drops 1 foot in 490 feet.

Speed Restriction Signs They apply where the line is under repair. First you will see the Advance Warning Sign (37), then, where the repairs actually begin, a circular notice repeating the speed limit and finally, where the repairs terminate, a large letter T.

Maximum Speed Notice (38) (39) Rather like the speed limit signs on our roads.

(35)
1/4
1/4
1
3/4
3/4
(37)
15
19
19
L
41
41
(38)
125
326
1
(35)
1/2
(36)
490
LEVEL

Whistle Notice (39) A warning to the driver to sound his whistle. You might also see the sign SW – Sound Whistle. It can stand for either whistle or warning since in fact trains have two-tone sirens not whistles. SPY it before the entrance to a tunnel too.

What trackside sign did you see? ....Score **30**

My sign was illuminated white on blue at ....

Loading Gauge (40) To check the safety limit in height and width of goods on wagons.

Catchpoint If a train breaks loose and runs backwards, catchpoints automatically turn it off the running track.

Line ahead under repair A white arrow inset with two yellow round lights: the figure on the top is the maximum speed allowed.

Summit Notice It gives you the height of the summit climbed.

I-Spy an engine driver exchanging tokens with a signalman.

Tokens are staffs with a leather loop at the end. A driver must have one in his possession when working on a single track which is used by trains going in both directions. It proves there's only one train on the single line, and is a protection against accidents.

Here's something else to watch out for – tracklayers' or lengthmen's huts. You will see several different types.

How many of these huts do you pass every mile or so on your journey? .... Score **60**

10
W
(39)

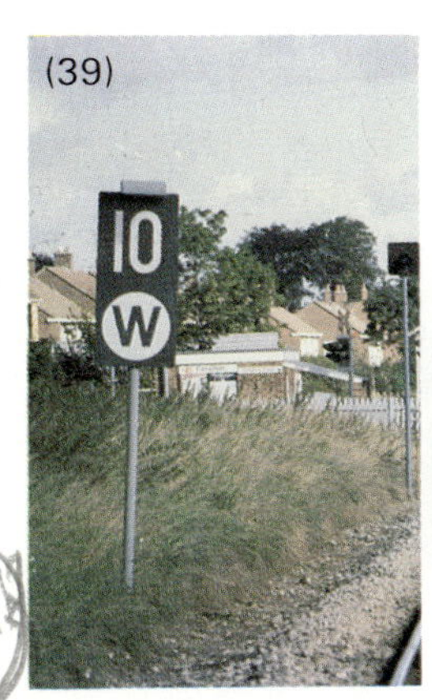

(40)

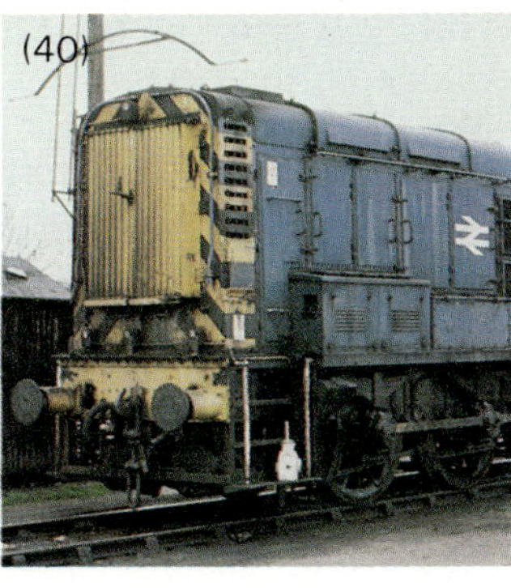

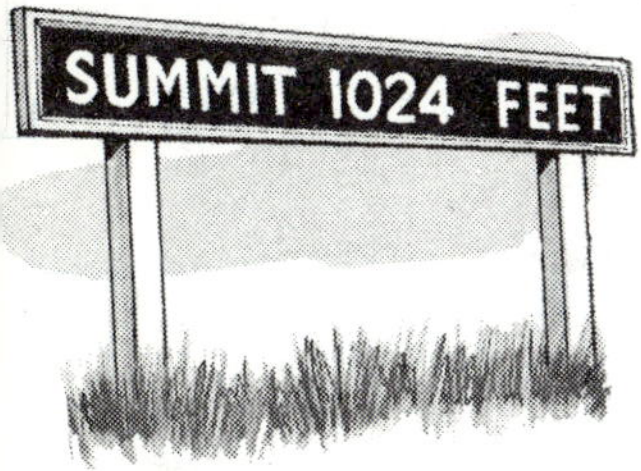
SUMMIT 1024 FEET

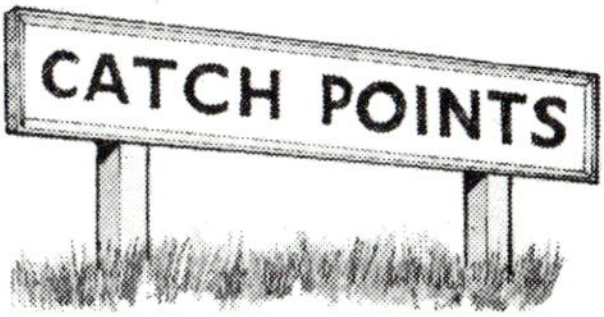
CATCH POINTS

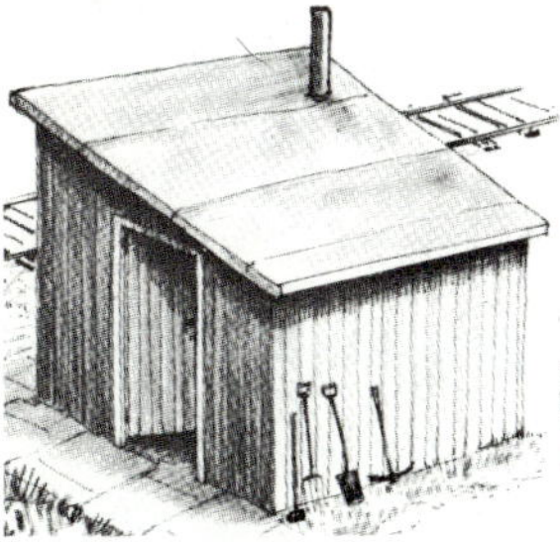

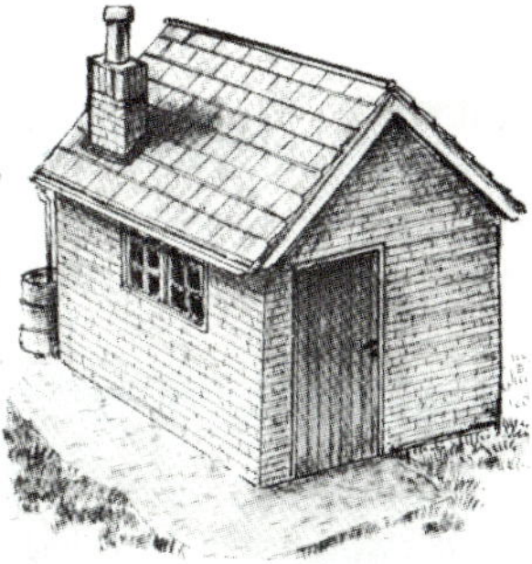

What you can see beyond the railway

Wildlife on the banks

Since no-one walks on the railway banks, the wildlife flourishes undisturbed. Often this means it gets covered by bushes and small trees, but you should also see Wildflowers and some Wildlife if you are very lucky. (There are I-SPY books to help you on both these subjects).

I-SPY primroses in flower in early Spring ....Score **30**

I-SPY a rabbit .... Score **15**

Industry

I-SPY industrial plants, tall chimneys, factory or giant cooling towers of a power station (41).

What did you see that most interested you? .... Score **30**

Watch for bridges, which you will go under and over. (42) is the oldest cantilever bridge in the world, carrying a modern train.

Which bridge is it and what is the train?............ ....Score **20**

Bridges can be arch or beam bridges (43), mostly made of brick and stone.

Which kind of bridge did you see? ..... Score **10**

You will see too a disused branch line, sometimes the track has been taken up, but also look out for rusty tracks a sign that they have not been used for a long time.

(41)

(42)

(43)

A very important role for the railways is the transport of freight. A lorry can carry up to 30 tonnes on one journey, a train can take 1000. In 1982 over 90 million tonnes of coal was transported by rail. The train (44) is taking coal from the mine to the power station. It is called a merry-go-round because the coal is dropped into special wagons at the mine, and tipped out again at the power station while the train is still moving.

Freight is also carried in wagons owned by large companies (45). The train is pulled by a British Rail loco, but the maintenance of the wagons is often done by the company. Oil is carried in tanks, painted in the colours of the oil company which own them.

Which company wagons did you see? ....
....Score **20**

Freightliner trains take containers (46). You may see different types of containers: each train may have up to 20 wagons – possibly 25 wagon trains may be introduced. Containers may be 3, 6, 9 and 12 metres long. They are loaded at factories, brought by road to the liner train terminal and put on special flat wagons. Long distances – say London to Glasgow – are covered at speeds of up to 120 kph.

What was your freight train carrying? ....
....Score **50**

Cars on wagons (47) are new ones coming from the factory. When you want to take your car on the train by Motorail, the cars are in covered wagons.

(44)

INTERFRIGO
ZEEBRUGGE
14 RIV-F
(46)

Cartrain
(47)

British Industrial Sand
(45)

Cuttings and embankments

Cuttings (48) and **embankments** (49); the work of the *navvies*, great teams of labourers who dug out the railways in the 19th century. They were called navvies because they 'navigated' the railways.

Through cuttings you can see how the batter varies with the type of earth – batter is the angle of slope necessary for stability. You'll also be able to see how rock and soil vary from one part of the country to another. Where it cuts through rock you might be lucky enough to see strata or layers of rock.

Bridges and tunnels Modern footbridges are made of concrete. Look out for viaducts, old bridges, motorway bridges and more.

Look carefully for a cast iron number plate, something like this one, fixed to the buttress of each bridge. It is useful when reporting defects for repair. You may also see a similar number plate on the wall at a tunnel entrance. By the way, there are 1,050 tunnels on the railways of Great Britain (50).

Approximately where was the tunnel you went through?...It was by a hill...........................

....Score **40**

Some tunnels have elaborate entrances, such as a pair of towers at each side. Tunnels are expensive and difficult to build and many navvies died from accidents during their excavation. If there is a churchyard near a tunnel entrance you may find some graves of those who died in this way.

(48)

(49)

(50)

Rails
(51) shows the Pandrol clip fastening on the standard flat-bottomed rail, now used on sleepers as standard track of main line. The points taper can be moved by the signalman in extremely cold weather because the gas heater unfreezes the points. There are about 14,950 heaters in use which can be operated by town gas, propane gas or electricity. Gas heaters are becoming rarer as they are not so safe. They can be recognised by the cylinder by them.
I-SPYed a heater at ....
....Score **30**

Adjustment switches (52) expansion joints on long-welded rails. Steel expands in hot weather, contracts in cold. In the old 60 feet (14.7 metres) track every joint has an expansion gap; hence the familiar rhythm as the wheels pass over them. In long-welded track these gaps disappear – and so does the familiar noise.
Track Indicator An automatic warning system. A small ramp, containing magnets, is fixed between the rails near the distant signal. The magnets set off a receiver in the locomotive and helps the driver by telling him if a distant signal is clear or caution.
Where did you see a track indicator? ....
....Score **70**
Other things which look after the rails are snow ploughs, de-icing units (in converted carriages), water cannon trains which blast leaves off the lines in Autumn.
Score for any of these .... Score **50**

(51)

(52)

Maintenance
Diesels are stored and maintained in depots. Most depots have long inspection pits between the lines for easier maintenance. You may see a diesel being cleaned; it is slowly moved between strong jets of water. You may also see carriages being cleaned in the same way.

Permanent way men All sections of track have to be continuously maintained. A group of track-layers – or lengthmen – work together (53). The man in charge is the ganger, who has a sub-ganger to help him. There is always a look-out man who warns the gang, usually with a horn rather like a huntsman's. Maintenance men wear bright 'dayglo' jackets, and trains have their fronts painted bright yellow so they can be seen more easily.
Where did you see a gang working? ....
....Score **40**
(54) shows a **tamping machine** used for re-laying track and also for maintaining track already in position. It packs ballast tightly round and under the sleepers so that they do not move when trains pass over them. There is also a machine which lifts the ballast from the track, cleans and re-lays it.

Other unusual machines you might see are a track recording trolley which discovers, measures and records faults in the track; a weed killing train which can spray the track and embankments with chemicals.
What unusual machine have you seen? ....
....Score **50**

(53)

(54)

Level crossings

There are many kinds, old (55) and new (56).

With the exception of crossings where there is little rail and road traffic, all modern crossings have traffic light signals – an amber warning light and red flashing STOP lights – together with an audible warning. Many have barriers.

You must STOP when the lights show.

NEVER Zig-Zag round barriers.

Automatic half barriers (56) have traffic lights and half road-width barriers automatically operated by the approach of a train. Cross only when no lights are showing and the barriers are fully raised. For pedestrians there is also an audible warning; do not cross when the lights are on or the warning is sounding.

Automatic open crossing has no barrier, only traffic light signals.

Open crossings without barriers or traffic light signals – are found where there is little road or rail traffic. At this crossing you should treat the railway as a major road. You must look out for trains and Give Way to them.

Traffic light signals are always provided at crossings where there is more than one railway track and more than one train may be crossing or about to cross. When this happens the red traffic signals will continue to flash and any barriers will stay down until the crossing is clear. Look out for barriers with skirts, or cattle and trespass grids.

What kind did you see? .... Score **20**

(55)

(56)

Old railways (58)

All over the country there are private organizations which run, maintain, and preserve old steam trains. they are run by very enthusiastic volunteers, who give all their spare time. The public can go on the trains and visit museums which are full of exciting things to see. Write to the Association of Railway Preservation Societies, Sheringham Station, Norfolk if you don't know where your nearest steam railway is. (59) Volunteers are rebuilding extra miles of line for the Kent and East Sussex Railway in Tenterden, Kent. (60) is their badge. Each railway had its own badge until they joined into one big organization, British Rail, in 1948. Look out for these badges at old stations.

What railway relic have you seen? .... Score **100**

As well as introducing super-speed passenger trains British Rail has also re-introduced 'steam specials' – in a small way at least. 15 stretches of line have been chosen for the operation of steam-hauled excursions. The routes are: Birmingham to Didcot (77 miles), York to Scarborough (42 miles), Carnforth to Barrow (28 miles), Dundee – Dunfermline – Cowdenbeath – Dundee (circular 91 miles), Carnforth to Leeds (64 miles), Barrow to Sellafield (35 miles), Guide Bridge – Dore – Sheffield (40 miles), Tyseley to Stratford-on-Avon (22 miles), Newcastle – Stockton – Middlesbrough (48 miles), Hatton Lapworth to Stratford-on-Avon (9 miles), Edinburgh to Aberdeen (130 miles), Dundee to Edinburgh via Stirling (90 miles), York – Harrogate – Leeds (39 miles), Chester to Newport (136 miles), Manningtree to Ely (60 miles).

Where have you seen a steam train on the track? ....Birmingham.... Score **150**

Paignton, Devon.

(58)

(59)

(60)

Kent & East Sussex Railway

Old trains

The biggest railway museum is at York. You can see it from the window of the train going along the London–Edinburgh line. They have a large number of trains and many special exhibitions. There is the Furness Railway locomotive 'Coppernob' of 1846 (61). Or the GNR No. 1 (62) built in 1870.

Have you got an old favourite engine or train? .... Score **100**

Steam trains can have speed records. The Mallard for example managed 202kph down a slope in 1938, but such trains need more power for the same speed, need more looking after and take a long time to warm up at the start.

Also in the museum is one of the most advanced trains yet built – the experimental Advanced Passenger Train or APT-E (63). It reached a speed of 240kph, and was fitted with special brakes, using water turbines. It had a gas-turbine engine similar to those of an aircraft.

An electric prototype version is now undergoing trials and may be seen on the Glasgow–Euston line.

I saw it on .... Score **80**

Opening and re-opening of station and routes

Since 1962 British Rail have opened or re-opened 83 stations. And more routes have been added – usually re-opening passenger traffic of lines still open for freight. Some stations have even been moved.

(61)

(62)

(63)

If you had this view on your train journey you'd know exactly how fast you were going. You'd be in the driver's cab and would be able to look at the speedometer. But how can you tell how fast your train is going by looking out of the carriage window?

You can estimate the speed of your train by looking at the mileposts which appear usually every ¼ of a mile. If your watch has a second hand find out how many seconds it takes for the train to travel a ¼ of a mile – that is from one post to the next. Then divide that number into 900. The answer is the speed of your train in miles per hour.

At what speed did you time your train? ....
....Score **50**

JOIN THE I-SPY CLUB

- All you need to join the I-SPY Club is to buy a Membership Book which includes the secret codes. Ask at your bookshop or newsagent.
- Tell your friends about I-SPY. Invite them to join and form a Patrol with you.
- Collect all the I-SPY books—and you'll have a wonderful library of your own.
- Write to me about any interesting discoveries you make. You may win a prize! Remember to enclose a stamped addressed envelope for a reply.

LOOK OUT FOR THESE I-SPY WITH DAVID BELLAMY BOOKS

AT THE AIRPORT
ARCHAEOLOGY
AT THE ART GALLERY
BIRDS AND REPTILES AT THE ZOO
BRITISH COINS
BRITISH WILDLIFE
ON A CAR JOURNEY
CAR NUMBERS
CARS
CIVIL AIRCRAFT
CREEPY CRAWLIES
DINOSAURS
FISH AND FISHING
FRUITS AND FUNGI
GARDEN FLOWERS ALL THE YEAR ROUND
GARDEN BIRDS
MAMMALS AT THE ZOO
ON A TRAIN JOURNEY
TREES
WILD FLOWERS

AND MANY **MORE!** TO COME

INDEX

ACKNOWLEDGEMENTS

Photos: Kent and East Sussex Railway (58-60); National Railway Museum, York (61, 62); Shell Times, page 2; British Railways Board, Public Affairs Department.

Published by Ravette Limited, 12 Star Road, Partridge Green, Horsham, West Sussex RH13 8RA

Printed by Brown Knight & Truscott Ltd. Tonbridge Kent
ISBN 0 906710 49 9